DEDICATION

This book is dedicated first to Jesus Christ, my Lord and Savior. I thank You, Jesus, for placing these words of encouragement in my spirit, for loving me when I didn't feel so lovely, and for encouraging me through Your Word. When I did not feel that I was educated enough to do anything for You, and when I felt like I had to know big words, You told me to "just make it plain," and that "big words have small definitions." Thank You.

This book is also dedicated to the memory of my parents, Mr. and Mrs. Butler C. and Mary L. Word, whom God used to bring me into this world.

To my spiritual leaders, Apostle William S. Rogers, Jr., and Prophetess Dr. Donna Rogers: Thank you for all your prayers and the strict teaching, and for your daring to be different. I love you, and thanks for the example you both set. Keep on keeping it real.

To my big sis, Ms. Nettie B. Harris: Thank you for always being there for me, for the listening ear, and the shoulder that I used a lot to cry on. Thanks for being there for me. I love you, sista.

To my friend and sister in Christ, Cynthia A. Utley: Thank you for all of the help you gave me and for the inspiration that just naturally flows from you. I thank God for you.

And last but surely not least, to my son Sharif T. Irons and my daughter Tamika L. Hall: You two have always been the joy of my life, my reason for living when I felt like ending it all. I thank God for you both, my babies.

KATIE M. WORD IRONS

TABLE OF CONTENTS

INTRODUCTION 5

CHAPTER 1: I AM MY SISTER'S KEEPER 7
   REFLECTIVE QUESTIONS 14

CHAPTER 2: BE STRONG MY SISTER 17
   REFLECTIVE QUESTIONS 21

CHAPTER 3: STUCK IN LIFE 25
   REFLECTIVE QUESTIONS 35

CHAPTER 4: HOLDING ON TO WHO I AM 39
   REFLECTIVE QUESTIONS 41

CHAPTER 5: SINGLE AGAIN, BUT NOT ALONE 49
   REFLECTIVE QUESTIONS 55

CHAPTER 6: AGAINST ALL ODDS 59
   REFLECTIVE QUESTIONS 73

CHAPTER 7: GROWING PAINS 77
   REFLECTIVE QUESTIONS 81

CHAPTER 8: QUEEN IN THE MAKING 85
   REFLECTIVE QUESTIONS 91

CHAPTER 9: CONCLUSION 95
   REFLECTIVE QUESTIONS 100

EPILOGUE 103
   REFLECTIVE QUESTIONS 107

MEET THE AUTHOR 110

INTRODUCTION

I believe that we all have a story to tell. There are things that we have experienced, the way we dealt with it and how we prevailed, that are like chapters to a book. If some of us took the time to share our stories, we could impact generations.

There are a countless many of us experiencing life in isolation. We sometimes feel that what we are going through, no one has ever experienced. Hence, we struggle, feeling alone and even abandoned. However, if ever given the opportunity to read a quote, a caption, something… we may be able to draw strength.

While, I don't claim to be an expert in the matters of life and I do believe that when we go through things in life we are suppose to learn something, and sometimes what we learn could save a life.

I wrote this book because I have a heart for women, all women, and when I use the term "my sister(s)" I'm referring to us, the sisterhood - all races, all ages and all stages of life, [as reflected on this book cover], we are connected. I am sharing some of my life's lessons that in hopes that it would help someone.

Have you ever read something and you were like - "Wow, that's the truth?" What you read spoke to you. It was a nugget that you will be useful for your and those around you.

A nugget may be small but it's something of value, it's precious. It may be one word or one sentence that you read in my book, I hope it encourages you to be strong and hold on to your hope.

This book deals with my life and lived experiences. I'm not an authority of life, but have garnered several nuggets along my journey. As I get older, I think more and I see things that I did and I realize that I could have done it differently I can't go back and undo it but that's a lesson learned that I will never forget.

Life is enjoyable, but sometimes challenging. I've embraced each challenge, and ultimately want everything that life has for me and I pray the same for you.

After each chapter are a few questions for reflection. Take time to reflection on life as it really as, and seek to go higher in all God has for YOU! All the best!

All blank pages are intentional

1

I AM MY SISTER'S KEEPER

A Charge to Keep

Cain asked the question, "Am I my brother's keeper?" (Gen. 4:9 KJV). That question was prompted by a question that the Lord had asked: "Cain, where is Abel thy brother?" Cain lied and said, "I know not: Am I my brother's keeper?"

This conversation took place after the very first murder had been committed: Cain slew Abel. Since that moment, Satan has set out to destroy man. His mission actually began before this, in the Garden of Eden when he tempted Eve - it was Satan's intent to destroy God's man. If he (Satan) can't cause a physical death, he will try to cause a spiritual death. Satan tries to cut all ties and connections that man has with God by causing sin to enter into man's life, because sin separates us from God. So, Satan sets out to tempt you. According to Webster's Dictionary, "tempt" means "to encourage or draw into a foolish or wrong course of action; to lure." If Satan can lure you back into your old sinful lifestyle, it separates you from a godly lifestyle - and spiritually stamping out your influence in major areas of your life like your home, your community and your place of worship. Those are three major areas that God wants to use you in! Satan's ploy or tactic is to cause you to get out of the will of God. When we walk not in the will of God we cannot fulfill the purpose He has for us, and that purpose is to be used for His glory. So, the enemy, that old devil, sets a plan in motion against the Child of God.

THE PLAN: DECEPTION AND SEDUCTION

First, let us establish the fact that the devil cannot make you do anything - that's a fact, and there is scripture to back it up. The Word of God said, "Behold, I give you power to tread on serpents and scorpions, and over all the power of the enemy: and nothing shall by any means hurt you" (St. Luke 10:19 KJV).

Now because people don't realize that they have been given this power to stand, Satan comes to their mind and makes a suggestion, and they often fall for anything and everything.

So Satan uses man's ignorance against him, and exploits his lack of knowledge concerning a thing. He (Satan) uses things like deception.

For example, a single sister may have a thought planted in her mind like, 'God made woman for man, so in order for you to be happy and complete you need a man in your life.' Well, it is true that God made woman for the man, so my married sisters submit to your own husband. But God's Word never stated that a woman must have a man in her life to be happy and complete.

There's nothing wrong with wanting a mate; that's a natural desire. God made us (women) to be helpmates, and that's what we do: we help. When your time comes you want the right person in your life, because marriage is actually supposed to be for life. The Bible said until death do ye part. But don't you run after the man. You stay hidden in the Word of God; don't compromise your stand and your time will come.

What you must understand is that God made us complete beings, lacking nothing. When God formed man out of the dust of the ground and breathed into his nostrils the breath of life, man became a living soul (Genesis 2:7 KJV); he was complete before he ever stood up! Praise God!

The revelation in those scriptures is that everything that we will ever need in life is already within us, like the tree that is within the seed. We just have to cultivate it! According to Webster's Third New International Dictionary, the word cultivate means "to cause to grow by special attention or by studying; practicing." II Timothy 2:15 (KJV) says, "Study to show thyself approved unto God, a workman that needeth not to be ashamed, rightly dividing the word of truth."

Satan knows the Word, he just can't live it. The deception is that he speaks half-truths to your mind, he tells you bits and pieces, just enough to sound like the truth. Do you know that a little truth mixed with a little lie is still a lie? That's why it's so important for you to study God's Word! That way, when negative thoughts are presented to your mind you can rightly divide and know whether they are of God.

God will never speak anything to you that cannot be backed up by His Word. You can be only deceived by your ignorance, your lack of knowledge.

Another device that Satan uses in his plan is seduction. He will entice you into wrongful behavior. You see, Satan just makes the suggestion; he speaks the thought to your mind and then waits to see if you respond and how you respond. It can be likened unto fishing: you bait the hook, throw it in the water, and then sit back and wait to see if a fish will take the bait. Sometimes the fish will take the bait. Sometimes the fish will nibble at the worm. Then other times he'll swallow it hook, line and sinker. And this is what your adversary is waiting for you to do. He's waiting for you to take the bait. You know - receive the thought, and then act on it. It's only when you act out of character that the enemy knows you've received the thought. You must learn to cast down imaginations, evil thoughts, and everything that would cause you to go astray. God's Word says, "Casting down imaginations, and every high thing that exalteth itself against the knowledge of God, and bringing into captivity every thought to the obedience of Christ" (II Corinthians 10:5 KJV). In case you didn't know it, you can send every evil, negative, and wrong thought back to where it came from. You bind it, cast it down, and send it back to hell where it came from, in the name of Jesus. Praise the name of the Lord! We have the right to do that, and when we do, we loose the things of God into our lives (See Matthew 16:19 KJV).

Deception and seduction are two devices in Satan's plan that he's using against the people of God in this hour. When we who are stronger in the things of God witness our sisters falling prey to the tricks of the enemy, we are to be our

Sister's keeper. We are to warn them and encourage them. We don't look down on them, nor do we condemn them but we love them back to their right standing with God. The songwriter *The Hollies,* penned the song, "He Ain't Heavy, He's My Brother," but God's Word said it like this: "We then that are strong ought to bear the infirmities of the weak, and not to please ourselves" (Romans 15: 1 KJV). The Amplified Version of the same verse reads - "We who are strong [in our convictions and of robust faith] ought to bear with the failings and the frailties and the tender scruples of the weak; [we ought to help carry the doubts and qualms of others] and not to please ourselves." We then who are strong sisters in the Lord ought to be able to put our wants and even our needs aside and reach out in love and help our weaker sisters who are struggling with some of the same things that God has already delivered us from and blessed us to come out of.

God never blesses us for us to shut up our bowels of compassion, but He blesses us to then be able to be a blessing to someone else.

Having gone through some trying times in my life, and knowing God delivered me through some major hurts and pains, there is no question that I must help someone who's going through some of the same things -my going through would have all been in vain. God does not suffer or allow us

I AM MY SISTER'S KEEPER

to endure trials and tribulations to keep us from encouraging our sister, and letting her know that she too can make it, because God is no respecter of persons. So then, the adage holds true: I am my Sister's keeper.

Reflections
Questions

1. Like the seed in the tree, like the Eve that was in Adam, what do you have inside of you that the world needs?

2. Recall the last time that enemy spoke a lie to you that you almost believed. How did you combat that lie? Or are you still believing its' "truth?"

3. Name some key areas in your life that you now have power over. How can you use these areas of strength to help your sister heal?

I AM MY SISTER'S KEEPER

Reflections

Reflections

2

BE STRONG MY SISTER

A Word of Encouragement

We as sisters in the body of Christ, especially us single sisters, sometimes feel like we're alone in this. Whatever our "this" is, Satan tries to suggest to us that we can't make it on our own, and he is right - we can't make it on our own, but "we can do all things through Christ which strengtheneth us" (Philippians 4:13 KJV). The *eth* in "strengtheneth" means God continues to give us strength time after time, after time.

Every time a situation arises in our life, God gives us strength to go through it. God never allows a test to come with the purpose or intent to destroy us; He allows tests in order to help make us strong. As long as you abide in the Will of

God, there's not a situation that will ever arise in your life that will overtake you. Isaiah 59:19b tells us, "When the enemy shall come in like a flood, the Spirit of the Lord shall lift up a standard against him." So be strong my sister because "There hath no temptation taken you but such as is common to man: but God is faithful, who will not suffer you to be tempted above that ye are able; but will with the temptation also make a way to escape, that ye may be able to bear it" (I Corinthians 10:13 KJV). And, again I say be strong my sister and know that regardless of what comes or what goes you can make it. I want to encourage you to be positive in all your thoughts and actions, and with whatever odds are against you, you can still make it. When it seems like there's no way out, you can make it. When you feel like giving up and going back - don't!

Don't give up and don't go back because you can make it. You may be in a situation right now and you don't know what to do. "Wait on the Lord: be of good courage, and he shall strengthen thine heart: wait I say, on the Lord" (Psalms 27:14 KJV).

I'm finding in life that it's an absolute must that we keep the right attitude - a good and positive attitude. When you think about it, the life we live is a result of the attitude we have. The dictionary defines attitude as "a state of mind or feeling," and we know that if we don't feel like doing something then we often simply won't do it. Our attitude is a byproduct of our thought life, the things that we think about on a regular basis. Thoughts are words that are sometimes never spoken, but they are real, and they live in our mind. They help shape our life. So, if you want to change your life, change your way of thinking – it changes your attitude. We need to start every day with words like, "I shall have a good day," and "I shall have good success." Psalm 118:24 said it like this: "This is the day which the Lord hath made; We will rejoice and be glad in it." We must learn to encourage ourselves when no one else is around.

Desire, like attitude, is also an absolute must. Desire is the motivation that drives you to do whatever it is in life you will accomplish. Desire is like the fuel in your automobile; the car won't run without the gasoline, and you won't move without the desire. You have to have a desire to get up every morning and go about your daily activities. It's the desire to have a roof over your head that motivates you to get up every day and go work an eight-hour job. If we really want to live our life for God, it's our desire along with the love we have for Him that causes us to stay on track. People who are married, must have a desire for one another to even stay together. And when we have an attitude of gratitude we can't help but be strong women in Christ – in our homes, in our communities, and in our churches. We become strong sisters producing strong sisters as we grow and encourage one another to "be strong my Sister."

I AM MY SISTER'S KEEPER

Reflections
Questions

1. List 2 areas that you view as weaknesses. Then list 5 areas that you see as strengths in yourself.

2. Recall the last time you needed to encourage yourself? What are times you need encouraging the most? How have you dealt with that?

3. Reflect on the last time your encouraged you encouraged someone else.

Reflections

I AM MY SISTER'S KEEPER

Reflections

KATIE M. WORD IRONS

3
STUCK IN LIFE
Choose Not to Stay There

Stuck in life: it's not a city, town, country, or area where you go to live. Instead, it is a state of mind, and it can be your place of "residence" (to dwell permanently; to abide; to live; to be vested in; as defined in the New Webster's Dictionary), if you so choose.

Stuck is just another term for being stagnant. Both words, stuck and stagnant, render the very same results. You cease to flow, become motionless, become dull - in your thinking and your actions - then over time you can become foul and end up with an impure heart. Matthew 15:18 (Amplified Version) states, "But whatever comes out of the mouth comes from the heart, and this is what makes a man unclean and defiles [him]."

When you're stuck (at a standstill) in life, it's like a baseball game where you are the only player. You have the bat and the ball; you stand at home plate, throw the ball up in the air, and then you swing at it with the bat. When you get a hit you have to run after the ball to retrieve it. And because the game has a whole nine innings to be played, you start the process over again…back to home-plate, hit, running after the ball, retrieving it…back to home-plate to start all over again…

That was even tiresome to read, wasn't it? Well that's a life that's stuck. It just becomes a cycle, and guess what? You're stuck. So now the cycle becomes your life. And the game has nine innings, you keep doing the same thing over and over again, and nothing changes because you're stuck. Other people want to help, they want to play in the game with you, but you're the one who has to pick your team before they can help by playing in the game.

The Opposing Team

What you don't see (spiritually) or realize is that there is an opposing team. The captain of the opposing team is the enemy of your soul, and he has no problem choosing a team for you.

So, he sends Insanity over, and Insanity comes with an impressive resume: He has the ability to affect a person with a serious mental disorder, impairing a person's ability to function properly. Now you're in a mental fog, thinking you can keep doing the same thing over and over again but get a different result - that's insane!

That's what insanity does.

Having other team players means having relationship. But you still don't want to pick a team, because a team has to function together in order to be successful. That means you, as the captain, have to share things about yourself that you really don't want to; as team players you need to know each other so the team can gel together. The better you know each other, the better you can function together as a team. Don't forget sisters, we need each other.

But you don't want your teammates to know your weak points, so you feel like if you don't pick team members you won't have to share your weaknesses or expose the areas that you struggle in.

Listen: what's in you, the weak areas, your struggles, and your issues have to be made manifest so they can be dealt with. It's how you get healed from whatever the issues are so you can move forward.

You think maybe if you just pick one person you won't have to share so much. But what happens is that one person you picked is waiting for you to tell them where you need them to help - you know, your weak area – and because you don't want to share too much, that person gets stuck also, because now that one player is trying to pitch and cover all the bases. So, the game (your life) still goes nowhere, and now you are both stuck in the inning with no end of the insanity in sight.

You have a teammate, but still stuck. The enemy of your soul, that old devil, has you right where he wants you - STUCK!

And not only that, but now you have someone else with you. You have a choice to make. You may be stuck but you don't have to stay that way.

It's a life or death situation!

Now if you want to stay stuck, the captain of the opposing team, the enemy of your soul, has a whole roster of names that he can send to sit your bench. He's got the Spirit of Heaviness who is one of his strongest players, and Heaviness brings with him Self-pity, Hopelessness, Dejection (disheartened; moody; in low spirits), Rejection, a Broken heart, Excessive mourning, Inner-hurts, Insomnia, and Suicidal thoughts. This is what the Spirit of Heaviness has to offer if you choose to stay stuck. Heaviness will load you down to the point where you lose your joy of living life. You'll start asking yourself questions like, "Why am I here?" and "What good is my life?" You'll start speaking and releasing negative words like, "I wish I had never been born," or "If I ran away no one would miss me." You need to realize that there is a spiritual attack against not just you but everyone - all of us are in a spiritual battle, and girlfriend we cannot afford to lose this battle. You have to come to a point in your life where you stand up and say enough is enough!

It's time. Come on, Princess Warrior. Enough is enough, it's more than enough. There's a way past that. Back in the day we use to say, "enough is enough, and too much stinks!" I know you're wondering where that came from, it's okay, as long as you get my point.

If you have reached this point in your life, come on, say it out loud, **"Enough is enough!!!"** No more overtime, no more extra innings; don't give the enemy of your soul one more foothold in your life. Take back all the ground you may have lost along the way and hear what Proverbs 6:13 (AMP) declares to you my sister: "But if he be found out, he must restore seven (7) times [what he stole]; he must give the whole substance of his house [if necessary-to meet his fine]."

Yesssss!!! I think it's necessary. Put a praise right there!!!

You have to refuse to forfeit the game. We don't give up and we don't turn tail and run. We have only one Judge who has the authority to pass judgment or hand out punishment and guess what, it's not the enemy of your soul, that old devil, Satan, your adversary - because his day of judgment is coming. As a matter of fact, he has already been judged. We have no reason to fear anything that Satan tries to throw at us, because he's already defeated; you just need to know that.

Champion, don't throw in the bat, the ball, or the glove. Square your shoulders, stand at home-plate, and realize that you do have the home-field advantage. Even Pastor Webster wants to preach on this. He said, advantage means, "any state of means favorable to some desired end; upper-hand; to profit; beneficial; opportune; convenient" (New Webster's Dictionary & Thesaurus).

The captain of the opposing team may have some strong players, but even they have to bow to the CREATOR of the Game, according to Philippians 2:10-11 (KJV): "That at the name of Jesus every knee should bow, of things in heaven, and things in earth, and things under the earth; And that every tongue should confess that Jesus Christ is Lord, to the glory of God the Father."

So, pick yourself back up and remind yourself that you're on Team Jesus! He has never lost a game, and He never will!

For everything that the enemy of your soul has tried to loose in your life by sending the Spirit of Heaviness, you bind it up according to Matthew 18:18a (KJV): "Verily I say unto you, Whatsoever ye shall bind on earth shall be bound in heaven." Then loose the Comforter, the garment of Praise, and the Oil of joy in your life according to Isaiah 61:3a (KJV): "To appoint unto them that mourn in Zion, to give unto them beauty for ashes, the oil of joy for mourning, the garment of praise for the spirit of heaviness." You have to use the Word of God and let it work for you - His Word is alive! Hebrews 4:12a (AMP) declares, "For the Word that God speaks is alive and full of power" [making it active, operative, energized, and effective]. Believe it and walk in it.

Victor or Victim, which shall it be?

I said in an earlier chapter that if you want to change your life, you have to change the way you think. Your mindset has to shift from being the victim to being victorious. Victory is yours, Champion! But you have to choose it, believe it, live it, own it, and walk in it. In other words, wear it like a tight-fitting jump suit.

There's only one option, and going back is not it. Do you

remember the account in the Bible of when God delivered the Children of Israel from their bondage in Egypt (Exodus 12)?

It was not an option that they could go back if they did not like their life in the wilderness. Isn't it something that when they were in bondage in Egypt all they wanted was to be free, because they had hard task-masters who worked them mercilessly? God heard their cry and sent a deliverer, and then once they were free, for a while, they wanted to go back to Egypt, which meant they would be going back into bondage! But that was not an option for them, and it's not an option for us now. We have a future, and we can't get to it looking back. Luke 9:62 (AMP) said this: "Jesus said to him, No one who puts his hand to the plow and looks back [to the things behind] is fit for the kingdom of God." So, if you don't want to die in your wilderness, whatever it may be, I suggest you get to stepping and keep it moving forward.

Make a bold declaration!

Years ago, I started writing scripture on post-it-notes, and I would stick them in places where I would be sure to see them every day.

Whatever I was dealing with or going through at the time, I would find scripture that dealt with the issue at hand and I would put them on my mirror in the bathroom and in my bedroom; I'd post them on the inside of the door that used whenever I left my house, so that the Word of God would be the last thing I saw as I left for the day. And at work I would write verses of scripture on scratch paper and place it in my desk drawer, so all I had to do was open my drawer and I could see the Word of God. I had gotten tired of always feeling like the victim, and I was going to do whatever it took, by any means necessary, to come out of that stuck situation and be free in my mind. I didn't want to live like the Children of Israel any longer; they were free physically but still in bondage in their spirit and in their minds. I told you, the mind is the battlefield and the victory is either won or lost in your mind.

You have got to make a bold declaration! Declare to yourself, the Devil, and whoever else is trying to block your way, that you are free, here to stay, and you're not going anywhere Announce that, "If the Son therefore shall make you free, ye shall be free indeed" (John 8:36 KJV). That's a post-it note moment! Make your mind up, and make a bold declaration to not forfeit the game or die in the wilderness.

Another thing: when God sends someone to deliver you, after you kept asking Him over and over, don't get in your place of deliverance and start talking about, "you wish," and "you remember when." Stop looking back in your mind and remember what Luke 9:62 had to say about that. Now I don't know about you, but I want everything God has for me.

Stay encouraged! Don't allow yourself to get stuck in life anymore, and keep moving forward toward your future and your destiny.

Reflections

Questions

1. When was the last time you felt stuck?

2. What did you do to overcome being stuck? If you are still there, what you can you do now to move forward?

3. Enough is enough! What areas in your life can you decree this in? Is it your finances? Your mindset? A relationship? Your negativity? What are some things you will end today?

Reflections

I AM MY SISTER'S KEEPER

Reflections

KATIE M. WORD IRONS

4
HOLDING ON TO WHO I AM

A Personal Testimony

Holding on with all you've got, trying not to get lost in the shuffle of life - it's hard sometimes trying to be who you really are. If you're not careful you'll tend to let people around you dictate to you who you should be, and you won't even be aware of what's happening.

I was married for twenty-one years before I got a divorce, and one thing I learned to do was to make the best of whatever life had to offer. That's not to say that was always the best thing to do, but it was what I did. It was not always easy to do - making the best of whatever, but I did it anyway.

I had two children and a strong determination to raise them the right way and be the best Mom that I could possibly be. I did not always do the right things, but I always had a desire to be good to my babies.

Through my marriage, I learned some valuable life lessons. I learned how to be strong and I learned how to let go. I rededicated my life to God in the midst of a lot of pain, frustration, and heartache, and I developed a relationship with God. I say developed because it did not happen overnight. According to Houghton Miflin's Pocket Dictionary develop means "to bring, grow, or evolve to a more complete state."

My faith had to grow, and I had to learn how to trust God with everything. That took time - a lot of time. Time on my knees in God's face, saying here I am again God; crying and wondering why or why not; receiving my answer and crying some more. It's when we come to the realization that we can do nothing without God that the trust is formed. And when we yield ourselves to Him, the relationship starts to develop. It's like a relationship between a husband and a wife. When you first meet that person, something about them attracts you to them, but you don't really know them so you don't trust them with all your secrets in the beginning.

But as your relationship develops and you get to know that person better, you open up more and more, and you start to trust them with your deepest thoughts; you let them into areas of who you are that no one has ever been allowed to enter. And when you develop a relationship with God, even though He's all-knowing, you start to open up, and you find yourself telling God all about your problems. You discover that He has the solution.

You know life has a way of happening to us all, and it's the things we go through in life that make us who we are. Situations shape our character; they either make us strong or they break our spirit and we become weak. I am a survivor, and the things I went through made me strong; they made me who I am today - a strong woman of God.

I don't claim to be an expert in the matters of life, but if you go through anything you should at least learn something -- and my desire is to share some of what I gained to hopefully help someone else avoid some pitfalls. I want to encourage you in what you're going through.

Because now, some things I know I won't do again; some paths I won't take again. It's like once you get burned, no one ever has to tell you not to play with fire again.

I also found that it is possible that you can lose your identity in a relationship, and that's not to say that when God blesses you with a spouse that you shouldn't give your all to the relationship, because you should. According to the Bible in I Corinthians 7:33-34, "the married careth for the things of the world, how he/she may please his wife/her husband," but God also created us individually and we are both to be unique beings, able to be used of God individually and together.

But if you're not careful and prayerful, you can get caught up in the relationship to the point where you lose your individuality. I almost lost sight of who I was. That may sound crazy, but it can happen.

When you get so caught up in trying to make your spouse happy, or trying to make everything right, or make things work perfectly for your spouse it becomes a never-ending job. I call it the "merry-go-round syndrome," because it never stops. It just keeps going around and around and around. It gets to the place where you won't even say what you feel or what's on your mind because you're afraid it will be taken the wrong way, and you'll have to deal with some kind of consequence. Have you ever been in a room with someone and you felt like you were not there? If so, then you know what I mean. You know the games people play.

I AM MY SISTER'S KEEPER

You are a wife, a mother, and a full-time employee. You start to feel like there are just not enough hours in the day, not enough of you to go around. There's no such thing as time for yourself - who is that anyway, "yourself?" Life seems to be on fast-forward and there is no slowing down. You're well on your way to being lost in the relationship.

Women, as a rule, tolerate more than a man will. We'll put up with a lot, and we take and take until we can't take anymore. When you get to that point, when you don't like what you see when you look at yourself -- then and only then will you begin to change. You will develop a desire to want to change, and you'll start to pray and ask God to help you change.

Perhaps you disagree that women will put up with more than men. It was true with me, and with a lot of women that I have talked with through the years. God made woman to be a helpmate and we are always trying to help things along. You know, trying to make it work.

Maybe you're reading this and you're going through in your relationship. I just want you to know that you don't have to lose your identity, and if you have you can get it back. You can be the woman that God created you to be. If you're finding it hard to forgive and move on with your life, I want to encourage you to let go of the hurt. Ask the Lord to heal you and to help you to forgive so you can go on with your life. Don't let your past rob you of your future.

Sometimes you have to change the things that you are doing. If you keep getting the same results that means that it's not working.

With me, my prayer changed, because I realized that no matter how bad I wanted the situation to change, I couldn't change it. You can change and you can do things differently, but it takes two people going in the same direction in life to cause a permanent change, and more than that, it takes both of you putting God first in your life. Only He can make a lasting change in the lives of men and women.

I used to think that I was a weak person. I depended on my husband and I felt like I couldn't make it without him. Can I just keep it real? I had lost sight of me and who I was, and I was trusting in man more than God, and we all know that won't work if you mean to live for Him.

Sometimes you need to stop and take an account of your life.

Who do you have first in your life? Is it God, or man, or things? If it's not God then I can tell you now that you're headed for trouble -the saints of old say, "You're headed for ship wreck." I had to put God back on the throne in my life.

I couldn't do it for my husband and he couldn't do it for me. You see, this is individual -- every man for himself. And by the way, you cannot make anybody happy, for happiness comes from within. My desire had always been that our marriage work, and that we serve God together as a family, but that didn't happen.

Time passed, and one day I found myself in prayer seeking direction. You must understand that you cannot do what everybody else does, and my solution may not be the solution for you, so you seek God for your answer. But no matter what you do, don't lose your identity, and if it's already gone, get it back. Get your identity back and hold on to who you are in Christ.

Reflections
Questions

1. Your journey may be different from mine, but what things have impacted your identity? Good or bad.

2. Identify situations in your life that may have cause disappointment. How did you recover?

3. Can you honestly say God has first place in your life? Above your job, your spouse, even your children, is God your primary focus? If not, what can you do to change that?

I AM MY SISTER'S KEEPER

Reflections

Reflections

5
SINGLE AGAIN, BUT NOT ALONE

Dedicated to My Sisters-Single & Divorced

I will lift up mine eyes unto the hills, from whence cometh my help. My help cometh from the Lord, which made heaven and earth (Psalms 121:1-2 KJV).

This is one of my most favorite scriptures in the Bible. In fact, it is one of the first verses of scripture that I memorized, and I used to say it over and over until it became a part of me. Friends and family are good to have, but they can't help me like God can. So when I didn't know what to do about a situation, I would apply this scripture. When I didn't know who to turn to, I would apply this scripture. When I felt like I was the only one going through, I would apply this Word. It always made me feel like I could make it another day, because the Lord is my help and I knew that my help came from Him. Then I read in the Word that if I "trust in the Lord with all my heart, and lean not unto my own understanding. In all my ways acknowledge him…he shall direct my paths" (Proverbs 3:5- 6 KJV). I began to grow up spiritually, and I grew to depend on God more and more, and less and less on man.

Life does not always seem to be fair. Sometimes it deals you a bad hand, and sometimes you're just reaping what you sowed. But you must hold on - and you have to hold on to what you know, not what you feel, because your feelings deal with the soulish part of you: your emotions, reasoning, and intellect. If you live by your feelings you will always be on an emotional roller coaster, up and down, in and out, and round and round. You have to base every decision you make on the Word of God. So hold on, don't give up, don't give out, and don't give in because the best is yet to come.

When the man Job went through all that God suffered him to go through, he never cursed God and he never left God, but he held on to what he knew and not what it felt like. I'm sure it must have felt like God had left Job when things started happening to him. His world was turned upside down, but you know what? God was right there. In fact, it was God who asked Satan the question, "Hast thou considered my servant Job?" (Job 1:8 KJV).

Maybe you're divorced and things aren't going right; your world seems to be turned upside down. Maybe you're right in the middle of a mess and you are not sure about what to do. Or maybe you just love the Lord and you want to live for Him, but nothing ever seems to work out right. Did you ever think that just maybe you're being considered, my servant? If you never go through anything you'll never know that God can bring you out.

You may say, "If I just had someone to help me make the decisions I need to make," or, "If I just had a man, a mate, or a strong arm to lean on, everything would be alright." Well, Job had a mate and she told him to "...curse God and die (Job 2:9 KJV). That is why it's so important to get in relationship with God for yourself so when those times of decision come (and they will), you'll know who to turn to, and who to lean on. A mate is good to have but make sure he's a saved man of God and in relationship with the Father. **Remember my sister, you don't find him, he finds you.** The Bible said in Proverbs 18:22 (KJV), "Whoso findeth a wife findeth a good thing, and obtaineth favour of the Lord." The "whoso" in this verse refers to the male gender and he findeth a wife, the female. So you stay hidden in Christ and let God send him to find you.

Having been married and now single again, the enemy (Satan) would have you to believe that you just can't live or make it without a man in your life. The enemy wants you to believe you have to have a man to be happy, or to feel secure and complete, or not to be lonely, or to be a total woman not wanting for anything, or whatever lie the enemy wants you to believe. You've got to know in Whom you believe or the enemy will wreak havoc with your mind. You must understand that the mind is the battlefield and the victory is either won or lost in the mind. "For as he thinketh in his heart, so is he." (Proverbs 23:7a). Don't let the devil or anyone else speak louder to you than the Word of God.

Where is it written that you have to be lonely just because you're single?

Take this time to renew your vow to the Lord. Get intimate, closely acquainted, and familiar with God. Get that real close relationship back that you had with Him when you first asked Him into your life. You can romance God like never before with no interruptions. Put the "do not disturb" sign out. Get engaged in a love affair with the lover of your soul. Lay out before Him and let Him hold you in His arms. Tell Him who He is and who He is to you: Jehovah-Jireh - the

Lord will provide; Jehovah-Nissi - the Lord my Banner, my covering; Jehovah-Shalom - the Lord send peace; Jehovah-Shammah - the Lord is there; Jehovah-Tsidkenu - the Lord our righteousness; El Shaddai - the all sufficient one, or the God who is more than enough; Almighty God, the God of Abraham, Isaac and Jacob, from everlasting to everlasting.

Worship Him out of your spirit-man and let Him fill that void that only He can fill anyway, while you're looking for love in all the wrong places. Fall in love with Father God all over again, and watch Him work on your behalf. He wants to give you the desires of your heart and all you have to do is walk upright before Him (Psalms 84:11c, KJV).

So, if you desire to be married or married again, the best advice I can give to you my sister, is to wait on God, let Him send the man to find you. **Please don't you go out there and try to make you a man because all you will do is make you a mess.** And you saved sisters: don't just get married and then get divorced 'just because.'

Don't go that route just because it's the American way or just because everybody's doing it. We live and govern our lives according to the Word of God, and God's Word said He hates the putting away, except it be for fornication (Matthew 19:9 KJV). So Sis, you don't have a leg to stand on, unless he was "knocking boots" with someone other than you; you know, 'bumping bellies,' 'doing the nasty,' 'getting his groove on,' and I'm not sure what else this generation calls it, but I think you get my point. Don't put yourself in a situation that you're not emotionally or mentally ready for. Marriage is serious business. It is to be a life-long commitment. I love you my sisters, and I'm just trying to keep it real with you. I'm talking to real people with real hurts and real issues in their lives, and I know you don't want anyone playing with you or your emotions.

Timing is everything! Sometimes we just need to pump the brakes and slow it all the way down, and while you're single or single-again, you might as well enjoy your life in Christ. Be sold out for Christ; He can fill the void in your life and you won't have to feel alone.

Isn't it something how you can be in a place by yourself but have Christ on the inside and be content even more so than if you were in a room full of people?

Remember: where you are in life right now is where you are suppose to be. I Corinthians 7:17a (MSG) says, "And don't be wishing you were someplace else or with someone else. Where you are right now is God's place for you. Live and obey and love and believe right there. God, not your marital status, defines your life."

I AM MY SISTER'S KEEPER

Reflections
Questions

1. Identify areas of where you are impatient. In what ways can you improve?

2. Describe your prayer life. How can you make it better?

3. Be honest, what voices are speaking louder than God's in your life?

Reflections

I AM MY SISTER'S KEEPER

Reflections

KATIE M. WORD IRONS

6

AGAINST ALL ODDS

You Can Make It

Philippians 4:13 states, "I can do all things through Christ which strengtheneth me," and remember the eth means God continues to strengthen you.

Have you ever felt like your life has come to a screeching halt? Seems like nothing's going right, and you do the one thing that you have heard for years in church that you are never supposed do: you question God! I just had this thought: how can you have a conversation with a person but you cannot ask a question?

In spite of whatever you were led to believe would happen to you, you took the big plunge and you asked the question, "Why God?" Why is my life so messed up? Why is this happening to me, and why at this time in my life? Why don't You (God) fix it? Why? Why? Why? And after asking, you wait for that earth-shaking answer that you feel you deserve, because after all, you did not ask for any of this stuff. And in the compassionate way that God has about Himself (and by the way lightening didn't strike for asking God a question), in His own way, in that still small voice by way of the Holy Spirit, God speaks to your spirit and tells you something so simple that it just blows you away because you have read it so many times in His Word. You asked why? He answers: I Corinthians 10:13, "There hath no temptation taken you but such as is common to man: but God is faithful, who will not suffer you to be tempted above that ye are able; but will with the temptation also make a way to escape, that ye may be able to bear it."

That answer blew me away. Isn't it something how the answer to all of life's questions are in the Word of God? We often don't recognize them as answers until we are right in the middle of one of life's situations and we ask the question, "Why?" In that moment, the Holy Spirit who brings all things to your remembrance (John 14:26) takes you right back to God's Word. So, that leads me to believe that within the Word of God lies the answer to every problem you'll ever encounter in this life. Praise Him!

I AM MY SISTER'S KEEPER

It wasn't until I went through that I knew I could go through, and you have to go through in order to get through. There's no magic wand, no hocus-pocus; just go through! Go through what you ask? Everyday life situations: A spouse taking you through, children acting like they have lost their minds, the boss on your job treating you wrong, the dog you had for years won't let you come in your own house, the cat wants to scratch you, the car won't start - you name it, it's happening.

The light bill is past due and your phone was just shut off...all of the above - everyday life situations. The enemy (Satan, that old devil) tries to use all of these things to beat and wear you down, telling you that you will never make it. Satan tries to tell you that life is too hard – "just give up; there's an easier way to make things work!" Satan speaks this to your mind. "Do drugs; they'll clear your head!" "Find you someone, anyone, to hook-up with; it'll relieve the frustration!" "Cuss your boss out; you'll sure feel better!" Well, all of this in a sense is true, but only if you're walking in the flesh and not in the spirit. What the enemy of your soul doesn't tell you is that there are serious consequences if you respond to his suggestions. Satan can only tempt you in your flesh; he can't touch your spirit: "For they that are after the flesh do mind the things of the flesh; but they that are after the Spirit the things of the Spirit" (Romans 8:5 KJV). All that Satan has to offer deals with gratification of your flesh. You know as well as I do that we don't want to have to wait for anything; this is a generation where we want things quick, fast, and in a hurry. If it doesn't come when we think it should, we'll do everything within our own power to get it or make it happen. But all you're doing is satisfying your soulish desires - your flesh. But the real you, your spirit-man, is left wanting for the spiritual things of God, and that leads to a failure to thrive spiritually. Your spirit-man gets weaker while the soulish part of you grows stronger. The body, your flesh, is led by the stronger part of you; remember we are a spirit, we have a soul and we live in a body: "So then they that are in the flesh cannot please God" (Romans 8:8 KJV).

There was a time in my life when I felt like if I didn't exist then everything would be alright. I wouldn't have to deal with the heartache any more; I wouldn't have to cry any more— I could just drive my car in the lake and end it all. I actually felt this way at one time. I was so hurt that I could not even think right. Relationships are mental and they can do a number on you. I had to stop and think; I had too much to live for. I had two beautiful children who needed me, and more than that God loved me, and He had not brought me as far as He had for me to die - not like that. For a moment I had forgotten that I am a survivor. I can't even swim, and I don't like that much water at one time, so I know that was the devil planting those thoughts in my mind.

He (Satan) waits until you're at your weakest, then he sets his plan in motion. He's the type that will kick you when you're down.

If you're going through something or you're in mental distress—don't make any major decisions. Because what you're doing is making life-altering decisions based on your emotions and what you feel at that moment. You'll do something or make a move that you might regret for the rest of your life. So if you're stressed, or if you're pressured, don't make any major decisions. When you act on how you feel you're in your flesh, and your flesh will get you in a mess every time. Pray, seek God, and wait. Then decide what your next move will be. Remember, apply the Word to every situation; ask yourself the question WWJD (What would Jesus do)? When Jesus was tempted in the wilderness after having fasted for 40 days and 40 nights, He used the Word: "It is written," and after a few more futile attempts by the devil Jesus told him, "Get thee hence, Satan" (Matthew 4:1-10 KJV).

And that is exactly what we must do: use the Word, then bind the devil and cast him out in the name of Jesus! You asked the question WWJD? This is your answer. Jesus didn't play with the devil.

Look at the Amplified version of verse 10: "Then Jesus said to him, "Be gone, Satan!"

It was during the last week of my married life that I needed to make some major changes, and I could not afford to make snap or hasty decisions. Whatever I decided to do would affect the rest of my life and the lives of all who were involved. I prayed and I sought the Lord for direction; it was not the time to ask friends and family or other people what they thought I should do. I needed to make a sound decision because it would change my life. I prayed and I waited for an answer, and when different doors began to open I believed that God had made a way for me. You may think, "What was so hard about deciding to leave a situation where there was emotional abuse, adultery, and a child by another woman?" It was timing; timing is everything. I did not want to leave, then not be sure and keep running back. I wanted to know that I had done all that I possibly could have done. I believe God gave my husband a chance to get it right while we were still together. I say that because it was 13 years later before I left. There were times that I wanted to leave, but I felt like I just couldn't go. But during that time I really grew stronger in my walk with the Lord. I learned that you cannot place anything or anybody before God, and that is what I had done. I had to repent to God and put Him back on the throne of my heart. During those 13 years, I backslid - I failed the test, and you know what happens when you flunk a test: you have to take it over. So, I went through the same test again, just with a different player. But God is so merciful. He kept me in my right mind through all of that, because you do know relationships are mental, don't you? People have lost their lives because of affairs; people have lost their minds because of affairs - never to be the same again. People have ended up bitter and full of hurt and hate because of affairs. But thanks be unto God, He kept me through it all and He healed me from all the hurt. That's why I can write about my experience, in hopes that it will help someone else make it through and encourage them to hold on and know that the best is yet to come: you can make it.

You know God has no respect of persons. If he did it for me, He can and will do it for you. Have you ever been backed in a corner with your back against the wall and you felt like you had no way out? It's times like that when you either get closer to God or you get farther from Him.

There has to come a point and time in your life that you want to make it - that no matter what comes or goes, you are determined to make it. Against all odds I will make it: that has to become your desire.

According to Webster's Dictionary desire, is "to long for; to wish; to crave; to request or ask for." And when you desire a thing in your heart it gets in your spirit and then it becomes a part of you. I am a survivor; my mother was a survivor, and that spirit to survive was passed on to me.

Growing up I watched my mom go through some tough times, and I really didn't know they were that bad until I got older and I would think about the things that had happened. I realized what she must have had to deal with.

This is not to take anything away from my father, because he had to be gone a lot of the time to find work. My mother was there all the time, and no matter how bad things got we children never really knew it. She always looked for the good in a person or situation, and she knew how to make the best of what she had. She called it "making do." I would see her every morning and every night on her knees praying and thanking God for what He had done for us. So being the youngest of 10 children, I had to be a survivor. Back in the day there was a song out by artist Jerry Bulter called, "Only the Strong Survive." The Bible says it like this: "I can do all things through Christ which strengtheneth me." (Philippians 4:13 KJV).

God is so awesome. You know how in the Bible Jesus taught many times using parables? If he talked to farmers, He'd use seeds and sowers to get His point across; if He talked to builders He talked about houses, one built on sand and the other on a solid rock. Well, I say God is awesome because even today He'll speak a parable to you and make a thing so plain that the only reason you don't get the point is because you didn't want to.

Let me encourage you to hang in there and don't give up because you can make it. Years ago, the Lord spoke a parable to me, and not only could I hear Him speak but I could see what He was saying to me.

You hear Him speak to your heart, but you see what He's saying in your spirit, and although it was years ago I can still hear and see what He said to me.

I am the mother of two children, so since I'm a mother God took what I was familiar with and spoke a parable to me using my oldest child, my son. This was during the time that I was going through in my marriage. God woke me up one night and brought to my mind the scripture in Philippians 4:13, "I can do all things through Christ which strengtheneth me." The Amplified version reads "I have strength for all things in Christ who empowers me [I am ready for anything and equal to anything through Him who infuses inner strength into me: I am self-sufficient in Christ's sufficiency]." And God, in real simple words. said, "You can make it." There was no thunder, no lightning, no loud earth-shaking voice from heaven - just that little still soft voice from within. I laid there, and my eyes filled up with tears.

The Lord used the first three (3) weeks of my son going to kindergarten.

I was a stay-at-home mom until my son turned two, and I went to work, but his grandmother was my babysitter, so it was just like he was home with me. It was harder on me when he started to go school than it was for him.

THE PARABLE

The first week - Every day I dressed my son, took him by his little hand and we walked one block to the bus stop where the school bus picked him up. This was our routine every day for five days.

The second week - I dressed him and took him by his little hand and I walked him to the end of our drive, and I would stand there and watch him as he walked to the bus stop and waited for the bus. I waved bye just before he climbed on the bus, and off they went. This was going really well, and I felt like 'I' could do this. But, about the middle of the second week we ran a little late one morning, and when my son was just about halfway to the bus stop the bus came. I told him to run, hurry up, run baby, and he started to run. He was giving it all he had, and he was doing real good until he tripped and fell. He started crying; I wanted to go and pick him up and bring him back home (I was hurting; Mama was upset) but I didn't move. All of a sudden, while he was still on the ground crying, looking at me, the bus driver threw open that door and started calling him by name. "Come on Sharif you can make it, come on Sharif!" She was waving him on with her hand and calling him, and then I started telling him, "Get up Sharif, run, you can make it, get up, you can make it, run!" And that little five-year-old boy got up, and with his scrapes and tears in his eyes, he ran as fast and as hard as he could, and he made it to the bus.

He stopped, turned, and waved bye and got on the bus.

My son had experienced a major setback, but he got up and he made it. We finished that second week out with me standing at the end of our drive.

The third week - I dressed him, took him to the front door, kissed him goodbye, and closed the door behind him. I'd watch him from his bedroom window and he'd wave bye with a smile on his face, and I knew he would be all right; I knew he could make it. And when I was going through a rough time just a few years later, God took those same three weeks and spoke words of encouragement to the very core of my being. He spoke those same words that bus driver herald at Sharif, He said, **"You can make it!"**

The Bible teaches that when we first get saved we are babes in Christ, and just like that first week of my son going to school, when I took him by the hand every day and walked with him to the bus stop, that's How the Lord does us. He takes us by the hand, and he leads us in the paths we should follow.

In the second stage, we are growing and getting stronger just like when I took my son to the end of the drive and just watched him walk to the bus stop by himself. God is with us, but He lets us go and He watches over us. And just like when my son fell one day during the second week, God said sometimes we may fall, but we don't have to stay down. Just like that bus driver was calling my son's name and telling him to get up, and that he could make it, that's how the Lord stands with his arms stretched out, calling us by name, telling us we can make it. And I was behind him telling him to get up, to run. Those are the people, the saints of God, that He has placed in our lives to help encourage us when we fall; they're behind us telling us to "get up, run, you can make it!"

And by the time the third week gets there we already know what it's like to face opposition. We've experienced a fall, we have a testimony—now we can step out a little farther, the same way I could take my son to the front door, let him know

I love him, and watch from the window. That's just like God: He always sees us, and now that I've gone through somethings I can tell someone else, "You can make it." Even though you fall sometimes, you can still make it. I know because I fell one day, but I didn't stay down; I got up and I ran as fast and as hard as I could.

I've been on my own (but not without the Lord) for some time now and I'm still running as hard and as fast as I can. Not once have I looked back with regret because of the decisions I've had to make. I put God back on the throne of my heart and there's not another worthy to take His place. I put my trust in God and not in man. I know I'm blessed because Psalm 84:12 declares, "O Lord of hosts, blessed is the man that trusteth in thee."

I would like to encourage you, my sister, to keep running. If you know the Lord as your personal Savior then hold on to Him, and never let go. By whatever means necessary, don't ever give up. Maybe you were running and you fell one day, and now you feel like "What's the use? I'll just fall again." I want you to know that you can make it, because you can do all things through Christ. Don't let the devil make you think that you'll never make it or that you'll never amount to anything. There is purpose for your life. If God loved you enough to call you out of darkness into His marvelous light there is purpose for you, and everything that happens to you or comes your way has to work out for your good. Hear what Romans 8:28 declares to you: "And we know that all things work together for good to them that love God, to them who are the called according to his purpose."

Against all odds, you can make it!

I AM MY SISTER'S KEEPER

Reflections
Questions

1. Maybe not physically, but when was the last time your fell?

2. How long did it take you to recover?

3. Do you have effective cheerleaders and/or accountability partners in your life? How often to you check in with them?

Reflections

I AM MY SISTER'S KEEPER

Reflections

KATIE M. WORD IRONS

7
GROWING PAINS
I've Been Stretched

Growing pains hurt for real. When God stretches you to get you out of your comfort zone, there's nothing you can do about it except go with the flow. Have you ever tried to just get through something, mind your own business, receive your healing so you can move forward with your own life, and leave other people alone…but for some reason it just doesn't work out that way?

The God we serve will do stuff that will have you scratching your head and asking the question, "Why are You doing this?" Really! He will stretch you far beyond where you thought you could go, and move you so far out of your comfort zone that you don't even believe you went there. When you tell God yes, that's when it starts: the stretching (to pull out; to reach; out; to be drawn out; to be extended; to spread).

We already know that the things we go through in life are not all about us, right? We know that God will allow us to go through things so we can help someone else; we understand that part of it. **Here's the kicker: sometimes the ones that we had to suffer for were the very ones that caused us the most pain in our life!** You know what the triangle looks like; it has three sides: you, him and them. When you get your deliverance you try to stay as far away from the people that caused you pain as you possibly can, and all alone God is setting you up to help those you are trying to avoid. You will find out in life that God's law of love has nothing to do with how you feel about a situation, and if you're going to be your sister's keeper you have to be willing to be used in very uncomfortable places in your life.

Did you ever imagine in your wildest dreams that God would use you to minister life and comfort to the third part of the triangle in your life? Well, me either, but He did. And know this: God doesn't just throw you out there and expect you to fail. Jesus said in Luke 22:32 (KJV) "But I have prayed for thee, that thy faith fail not: and when thou art converted, strengthen thy brethren." You can be somewhere trying to plead your case, telling God what He already knows: "But she...they...these are the ones that caused my heartache!" And your Heavenly Father who cares so much for you, whispers to your heart, "I know," and then he takes you to His Word in Matthew 18:14 where Jesus explains, "Even so it is not the will of your Father which is in heaven, that one of these little ones should perish." So you tell God "yes," and you go minister His love and peace and comfort to a person who caused you so much pain, and it's okay. Remember the Bible said, "For if you love them which love you, what reward have you?"

God will use your past hurts to bring healing to someone else, and we can't dictate to Him whom to use us for or whom to send us to. He said all souls are His, even the ones we call our enemies.

He had me to show kindness to a person, and I knew she had been the other woman (the third part of the triangle). This is what I mean when I say God can do some stuff that will have you saying, "REALLY?!" But those are the times of stretching, of pulling you out of your comfort zone so you can see that you've grown, because He already knows that you'll pass the test.

Jesus said in Matthew 5:44, "But I say unto you, Love your enemies, bless them that curse you, do good do them that hate you, and pray for them which despitefully use you and persecute you." That verse of scripture lets you know that it's really not about how we feel; it's not even about how a person may feel about you. Jesus said, love them, bless them, and pray for them - no excuses.

Remember, uncomfortable places in life cause growing pains, and it hurts when we are being stretched but it's all a part of the process.

If we don't go through the process we will never grow, and if we never grow we become stuck in life, and once we get stuck we become stagnant.

Stagnant means to cease to flow; to be motionless; to be dull; foul; impure (New Webster's Dictionary). So my sisters, keep growing and flowing in the things of life. Live life to the fullest get everything that it has to offer. Keep your hearts pure and keep love for one another as we grow together.

I AM MY SISTER'S KEEPER

Reflections
Questions

1. When was the last time you were forced outside your comfort zone?

2. How did you respond? How can you do better?

3. What lessons have you learned when you face challenging circumstances?

Reflections

I AM MY SISTER'S KEEPER

Reflections

KATIE M. WORD IRONS

8

QUEEN IN THE MAKING

Diamond in the Rough

Q UEEN = the wife of a king, a woman sovereign (a ruler with supreme power; or authority) or monarch (a person who reigns over a kingdom or empire) (New Webster's Dictionary). In chess, she's the most powerful piece on the board.

This is for all the Princesses—the daughters of the King. What you're going through now is called being groomed. According to Webster's Dictionary, to groom is "to prepare for a particular position." And that is why you can't be like everybody else; that's why you can't act like everybody else. You can't run around acting like you don't know who your

Father is. You know, you can't mess up on purpose because you have a reputation; your good name is at stake. Proverbs 22:1a tells us, "A good name is rather to be chosen than great riches;" Ecclesiastes 7:1 says, "A good name is better than precious ointment."

Being groomed is just another term for being 'made.' We're all born babies but then we have to grow up. And it's the training, the teaching, and the nurturing that we receive that help us grow into adults. That's the natural aspect, and the spiritual works the same way. We have to be born into the body of Christ and we are called babes in Christ. Then we have to be taught the things of God the Father; that's why we need a spirit-filled man or woman of God as our pastor, so they can speak the things of God into our life. You must have a church home, because a baby will die if it's left by itself. It is by the hearing and receiving of the Word of God that we grow spiritually. The latter clause of Romans 10:14 states, "...and how shall they hear without a preacher?"

You must be taught in order to develop properly. Remember you are Queens in the making! You are a princess right now, daddy's little girl, but you're being groomed to reign as Queen! You're becoming a woman with authority in Christ Jesus, moving in the things of God, directed by the Holy Spirit. I don't think we realize the power that God has called us to walk in. That's why it is so important that our lives line up with the Word. We have to be yielded Vessels –Vessels of Honor.

When we yield ourselves to Father God and we ask Him to work on us, He begins to take out of us everything that's not like Him and everything that is contrary to His will. He puts in us everything that should be in us according to His Word. That proud spirit has to be broken; disobedience has to be worked out of you. If you damaged your reputation along the way, you have to live down the bad reputation.

Remember you're in the making because you've got to reign!

You go through a process, and during this process God will use everyday life situations to get you to where you need to be in Him. Isn't it something how God can use earthly events to bring about heavenly results?

Haven't you ever gone through something in your life, and it was a hard thing for you to go through - there were times that you actually wondered if you were going to make it through - but you didn't give up and throw in the towel; you held on with all that you had?

Those are the times of trials and tribulations that make you. God has a way of refining us, and it gets us to maturity in the things of the Spirit.

Isaiah 48:10 says, "Behold, I have refined thee, but not with silver; I have chosen thee in the furnace of affliction." You don't become what God would have for you to be overnight - you know, saved today, and perfect tomorrow! It's a process. It's a life dedicated and submitted to the Will of God. Be willing to go through. Remember that everything you will ever need in life is already in you; it's a time of cultivation now. Cultivation is just another word for 'working it.' When God put Adam in the Garden, He told him to "dress it" and "keep it" (Genesis 2:15 KJV).

Haven't you heard the saying, "practice makes perfect"? Work it!

That's all it means. You take the gifts, talents, and abilities that God placed within you, and you work with what you've got to develop it into what it should be. You do that by first giving it all back to God, and through fasting and prayer you allow Him to mold you just like that clay on the potter's wheel. Imagine the potter sitting at his wheel working with his clay, and in the process of his working the clay vessel becomes marred (Jeremiah 18:4) or spoiled. The potter takes the vessel with the flaw in it, and he starts all over again. He makes another vessel. Can't you see him looking it over very carefully, making sure there are no flaws this time? Because whatever the vessel is going to be used for, it has to be strong enough to withstand the pressure of its use. That clay is us, and God is the Potter, and life's everyday situations are the wheel. And during the process of life, if we will allow God to use the tests and trials, they will work the flaws out of us and the finished product will be vessels of honor - Queens fit for reigning.

As you submit to God and allow the process of your making, you will become the Queen you were created to be.

The characteristics of the finished products are below:

> (a) Worthy: the quality of a thing which renders it valuable or useful; relative excellence of conduct or of character; value.

> (b) Example: a pattern; a thing illustrating a general rule.

> (c) Virtuous: upright; dutiful; chaste, uprightness.[1]

These are simple words with simple meanings, but they are words that are to be sown into our very Spirit, that our faith might wrap around them to the point that we become pregnant and begin to birth lives flowing with worth, good

---

[1] All definitions are from New Webster's Dictionary.

examples, virtue, and integrity as we walk in the authority of our Queenship in Christ Jesus.

The word pregnant means to carry a developing fetus within the uterus or womb; another definition states "full of meaning or significance." As Queens in the making our lives should be full of meaning and significance.

Our lives are to be a reflection of Christ. When we are around people, they should not only see the love of God in our lives, but they should also feel the love of God flowing from us. We are supposed to make a difference in the lives of the people we come in contact with. In pregnancy, not only are we supposed to birth forth lives flowing with worth, good examples, virtue, and integrity but we are supposed to birth forth souls for the Kingdom of God.

The Bible calls it "bearing fruit" (St. John 15:8 KJV). God spoke a word in my spirit. He said "Queens in the making are like diamonds in the rough." They don't always look like what they are, but once they go through the process they come out sparkling precious stones. So be encouraged my sister, because just like the process doesn't last forever neither does the making. You'll always have trials as a growing process to get you to the next level, but you'll also have seasons of reaping the benefits of the process. Be strong my sister, my princess.

Reflections

Questions

1. Look in the mirror. What reflections of God do you see?

2. How has "process" made you better?

3. Describe ways you maintain your hope in the midst of being 'made'.

Reflections

I AM MY SISTER'S KEEPER

Reflections

KATIE M. WORD IRONS

9
CONCLUSION

The Bottom Line

"Then Peter said unto them, Repent, and be baptized every one of you in the name of Jesus Christ for the remission of sins, and ye shall receive the gift of the Holy Ghost."
Acts 2:38-39 (KJV)

After all is said and done, after the dust is settled and all the dark clouds roll away…the bottom line is, you need Jesus! The scripture said, "Repent." I want to admonish you, married, single, single again, whatever the case may be: it's not worth living in hell on earth and then dying and going to hell. You've read this book and maybe you can agree or identify with some part of it, but the bottom line is you still need Jesus! The scripture said, "Repent and be baptized…for the remission of sin."

Right now, take a moment and look at your life: where are you? Are you facing opposition, and don't know what to do or where to turn? If you're saved, you need to get back up again, repent, and get back in the race!

We fall down but we get back up, we don't stay down.

Maybe you've gotten caught up in a relationship, not married, but just caught up in a relationship that's going nowhere real fast, dating for years and he still has not asked 'the question!' You need to pack your bags and run, don't walk, to the nearest exit. Let me ask you a question: do you want more from your relationship? Or are you okay with shacking, sharing, or playing house—you know, being the cow where he gets his milk free?

I'm not calling anyone a cow, but you have heard that old saying, haven't you, "Why buy the cow when you can get the milk free?" He can buy a collar for his dog and put it around his neck, and pay for his full-blooded dog to be registered, but can't buy a ring and ask you that simple question. What's wrong with this picture? Maybe it's just me…but he can't have any free milk or free cookies! Beyonce even sang a song about it: "Single Ladies (Put a Ring on It)." I Corinthians

6:18 said, "Flee fornication," and I Thessalonians 5:22 says, "Abstain from all appearance of evil" – you can't be looking like you're married.

So, let me back-up and rephrase that previous statement I made: if YOU are tired of the relationship that seems to be going nowhere, and the two of you cannot come to an agreement – you want a ring on it and he doesn't, then you need to cut your losses and move on. Repent, and ask God to sever the soul- ties that have been formed. Or maybe you are married and you're in a relationship where it seems like all hope is lost, adultery has been committed, maybe emotional abuse, or physical abuse has occurred. You may feel like you can handle it, and maybe you can, but if children are involved you are responsible for their wellbeing and safety. A bad relationship affects everyone in the house.

No one can tell you what you should or should not do, but I will say this, seek God because whatever your situation is and no matter what you're going through, God has a solution for you.

Maybe you feel like you have to take everything and just smile and say the Lord will make a way somehow. Well, that day is over my sister, it's a new day! The Bible said in Matthew 11:12: "And from the days of John the Baptist until now the Kingdom of heaven suffereth violence, and the violent take it by force." Every inch of ground that Joshua got he had to take. I'm not saying go out looking for a fight because it's all spiritual anyway, but what I am saying is don't let life kick you in the butt and you don't kick back. It's spiritual. You have to learn how to fight in the spirit; it's called spiritual warfare and it's real! Life is supposed to be lived, not feared or tolerated. You know, just putting up with stuff. Jesus said, "He came that we might have life and that more abundantly" (St. John 10:10).

So, after all is said and done, if you don't know Jesus you need to get to know Him. Invite Him into your heart. The scripture still said it: Repent!

My prayer is that after reading this book you have been encouraged by something I shared, that God dealt with you about your situation, and that you received answers to questions that you had. I pray that some light was shed in areas of your life that you thought were over. I pray that you be loosed and set free from ungodly relationships. I ask the Lord to touch and heal your broken heart, all the hurts and disappointments.

I pray, Father, that you touch the lives of all the children that were scared and hurt and broken in the bad relationships that they didn't even ask to be a part of. Pour the oil and the wine in the wounds of the hurting mothers and fathers, both single and married. God, let your peace that passeth all understanding rule in the lives of your people; let not one person that reads these words of encouragement be the same ever again. Change their life; cause them to be able to live again in Christ Jesus. God don't let the children be bitter, but take them in your arms and rock them and love on them. Lord You be that father they never had; You be that mother that they needed. Do a new thing in them. In Jesus name I pray, **Amen.**

And if you are not saved or you're in a backslidden state but you want to be saved and in relationship with Christ, and you want Him to be the head of your life, the scripture said repent, and then ask the Lord to come into your heart and live in you. *SAY IT OUT LOUD: "LORD JESUS, I REPENT OF MY SIN AND I BELIEVE YOU ARE THE LORD AND SAVIOR OF THIS WORLD. COME INTO MY LIFE."* If you mean what you say, He will do just that. Remember, He is faithful to His Word.

Reflections
Questions

1. Do you understand what it means to be saved?

2. Who are you in God? Do you understand your spiritual gifts?

3. Do you attend a bible-teaching church? How active are you?

I AM MY SISTER'S KEEPER

Reflections

Reflections

EPILOGUE

On a Personal Note

Whenever God puts a dream in your spirit and it seems so big that there's no way that you could ever accomplish it - you are absolutely right, you can't do it on your own. But with God all things are possible.

We serve a great big God and even when He puts a dream or vision in your heart, He's stretching you. He's trying to pull out of you what He already knows you can do. We just have to have the faith to believe that He will bring to pass everything that He has spoken concerning us.

God will never force us to do anything that goes against his nature, but if we just make that first move - you know, like the toddler that's trying to walk for the first time; they have to take that first step or they'll never learn to walk on their own, and after so long the toddler gets too heavy to carry. God will carry us for so long and he keeps nudging us along, but after a while we have to catch the vision and run with it or that dream will die in us, and we'll never be or do what God intended for us in our life time.

I didn't want the dream that God gave me to die in me, and that's why I pulled these written pages out and dusted them off. You see, God put this book in my spirit and heart years ago, and I would sit and write for hours at a time. But I would tell myself that I'm not a writer or an author, and no one wants to read these simple little words that I've written…who am I anyway? That's how I used to feel; I know better now. A short time ago God stirred my spirit again, and I really believe it's now or never as far finishing this book and getting it published.

I met a very nice young lady by phone and she said something to me that sparked something within me. She said our writings - our books -are legacies that we leave for our families and those who come along behind us. She said just think if the men of old had not written the scriptures as God inspired them; we would not have the Bible today.

Now you know I had to look up the word legacy. If you've read any part of my book, you know I am going to give you scripture and definitions because God told me a long time ago to "just make it plain." Legacy means personal property, money, and other valuables that are bequeathed by a will; anything that is handed down from an ancestor, predecessor, or earlier year; (Webster's Dictionary). And the Bible teaches us that a man should leave an inheritance for his children and his children's children.

We need to leave a legacy.

I didn't want to die with this book locked up inside me. If one person reads it and something I've shared helps them in any way, then what I have gone through has not been in vain. We have to get past the fear of rejection and whatever other road blocks and distractions the enemy or we ourselves have put up.

A lot of you have dreams and aspirations. Keep moving toward your dreams; never stop. Remember if you stop moving you get stagnant, dull and foul, and when you get foul you stink (it's spiritual).

You won't move, and you'll start to resent anyone else who is determined to move forward.

If no else supports you, you be your own biggest supporter - get your post-it notes out and start posting encouraging words to yourself.

I'm telling you those post-it notes work, and when you start speaking the words out loud to yourself, over and over every day, it gets in your spirit you start "calling those things which be not as though they were." That's the latter clause of Romans 4:17 (KJV).

Don't let your dream die in the fetal stage - still inside you. You have carried it long enough, your nine months are up, it's time to deliver this baby.

I can't encourage you to do something and not practice what I'm saying myself. So, I say to my dream as you speak to your dreams, it's time to come to pass.

Always remember that you can make it. This is not the end, it's the beginning! God bless you my Sisters, my Princesses, and God's Queens.

I love you all. From my heart to yours.
♥ *Katie M. Word Irons* ♥

Reflections

Questions

1. List some of your dreams.

2. What things are preventing you from pursuing them?

3. Do you understand that you're not getting any younger? And that God gave each of purposes when we were in the womb of our parents?

Reflections

I AM MY SISTER'S KEEPER

Reflections

KATIE M. WORD IRONS

MEET THE AUTHOR

Katie M. Word Irons. Life has been her greatest educator. What she has experienced in life, the mistakes she made and learned from, love and loved ones that she had in her life and lost, all taught her lessons that you cannot learn from a book or in a classroom. She remains grateful for what life has taught her.

She is the mother of two: Sharif (Deiardre) and Tamika (Xavier); Grammy to five: Shaizaka 'Shai', Renoni, Naomi and the twins Kaleb and Kendel, one great-grandson Shaizaka Jr. *I Am My Sister's Keeper* is her first book.

Visit her website for more information
www.katiewordirons.com

Made in the USA
Columbia, SC
11 June 2018